Why Me?

Why do bad things happen to good people?

Zehra Mahoon

The author of this book does not dispense any form of medical or psychological advice or prescribe the use of any technique as a form of treatment for physical, emotional, or medical problems without the advice of a physician, either directly or indirectly. The intent of the author is to offer information of a general nature to help you in your search for emotional and spiritual well-being. If you apply any of the techniques offered in the book, the author and the publisher assume no responsibility for your actions.

Why Me?

Why do bad things happen to good people?

By Zehra Mahoon

There is much appreciation here for everything I have learnt from Abraham. Everything in this small book is based on the teachings of Abraham by Esther and Jerry Hicks.

Zehra

Why I wrote this book and why you should read it

Very long ago I was confronted with a situation in my life, that I didn't think I deserved at all. I was in an abusive relationship, and eventually ran away from home at two months pregnant. The recurring question in my mind was "what did I do to deserve this?"

I had always been a "good little girl" who always listened to mommy and did what was right from a societal point of view – so how could I end up in this situation – how could God put me through this?

I observed a disparity in many cases – it did appear to me that life wasn't fair, but God was always supposed to be fair – so it felt like there was a missing piece, because things really didn't make any sense.

I've spent a lot of time thinking and sorting it all out since then.

This little book is meant to give you a glimpse into what I've learnt and how since then I have turned my life around completely.

I have peace within. I have joy in everyday of my life. I have learnt how God's system of granting wishes works, and I want you to learn how to use too. It makes me happy to know that I have made a difference. So if you find benefit in this writing, remember to send me an email or simply write a comment about this book.

Much love and appreciation

Zehra

Why Me?

Why do bad things happen to good people?

The Law of Attraction has an explanation for everything. Yesterday, I had lunch with a young friend who was full of questions. One of his questions was "if something bad happens – for example, someone gets a heart attack, when they had never ever thought about a heart attack and were perfectly healthy – how does the Law of Attraction explain that?".

I thought that the discussion he and I had was quite useful so I wanted to share it with my readers. This question is one I have encountered many, many times, and I think it is important to understand the answer, because clarity on this subject leads to clarity on all things.

I am reminded of the question: **"why do bad things happen to good people?"** –

to me it is really the same question. I am going to attempt to answer this question with the help of concepts I have learnt from Abraham.

There are three factors that play a role in something unwanted happening seemingly out of the blue: beliefs, emotions, and habit of thought.

So how is it that these factors play together to produce unwanted manifestations or results?

Each of us has a number of beliefs that we have picked up along the way over the years. Some of these beliefs are empowering, eg., "I can have, be or do anything I want" if you really, truly believe it and live it, it is an empowering belief. A lot of us offer the words, and would like to believe this statement, but often times, we have a little voice inside that is saying things like "yeah sure! If you could have anything you wanted, would you be living in this house, driving this car, with this bank balance etc, etc, etc...".

There is a disconnect between the intellectual knowing and the emotional accepting of empowering statements.

These statements and whether we accept them is reflective of our underlying beliefs about life.

We accept things based on our own life experience and link events and results based on cause and effect – just like the popular Pavlov's experiment with dogs. One day I went fishing with a friend. I don't fish myself, but it is meditative to be out on the open waters so I love going anyway.   He wore a very bright red shirt – I couldn't help remarking on the color. "You're going to scare the fish away with a bright color like that", I said meaning to poke fun at him. "I always have good luck fishing when I wear this shirt", he said, and then proceeded to tell me a couple of stories about the fish he had caught in the past. This was his "lucky fishing shirt" lucky only for fishing. Interesting how that belief got formed and then got reinforced? That's how it works every time.

There was a time a couple of years ago when I used to believe that I had to leave the house exactly at 8 am in order to avoid peak commuter traffic. I had to work on letting that belief go consciously in order to change my driving experience. Have you noticed how the person who expects to find crazy people on the road is the one who always has the wildest stories to tell? In my experience, people are nice and courteous and everyone wants to be safe. **People who fuss and worry are always the ones who have lots to fuss and worry about.** They create the expectation, based on a belief they have constructed and they prove it to be true every time.

So if we see evidence supporting a correlation between two events, we accept it, and if we don't see evidence we tend to discard it. Sometimes, we accept and take ownership of beliefs other people have constructed – of course, this is typical of children as they accept many of the beliefs their parents offer. Anyone who has power of influence in our lives can communicate their beliefs to us – but we don't always have to accept them. Accepting someone else's belief is a decision we make – sometimes consciously and sometimes without thinking.

Over a period of time we create a framework about cause and effect in our personal space – and the world we live in conforms to the beliefs that we have picked up along the way. **Therefore we limit the possibilities and the probabilities that could come to play in our lives.** If we did not have a limiting belief system the possibilities and probabilities that could come into play in our lives at any point in time would be limitless. For example, if I truly believed that money could come to me from anywhere, then the possibility that it could drop from the sky would still be a possibility that could be probable in my universe, whereas for someone who absolutely does not believe in such things, the probability of such an event would be zero. They would have eliminated the probability of the event in their personal frame of reference based on their beliefs.

Similarly, we believe in health related statements such as "my mother had cancer, so I must be more susceptible to it", or "people with a cold spread their germs – when you are exposed to the germs you get sick", "diabetes runs in the family". These are all examples of negative beliefs. A belief is a thought you think repeatedly and you accept as being true. The fact, that you accept them as being true, is what matches you up with evidence to prove your belief. That is precisely why one set of medical research proves that a substance is good for you and another set of research proves exactly the opposite. Happens with food all the time. For every set of research that proves a certain food is good for you, there is an equally convincing research available to prove that it is bad! Which set of research you come across depends on your own belief systems. Which set of research you accept also depends on your overall belief system.

Any negative belief that you hold on any subject becomes a weak spot in your vibrational make-up, so that when you accumulate resistance on that subject or on any subject at all, it shows up through that weak spot. Similarly, positive empowering beliefs create a shield around us that helps us deflect unwanted things.

Let me explain with the help of a few examples.

6

First, I will use the example of a dear friend whom I will call Jeanie. Jeanie suffered from a stroke almost four years ago. It was pretty severe and she was totally paralyzed on one side of her body. She has recovered substantially now and has the full use of her body. She attended one of my workshops last month, and her question was, "Zehra, I had never thought of having a stroke, so how did I attract a stroke?".

Jeanie is the most fantastic looking 75 year old I have ever known. At the time when she had the stroke she was perfectly healthy, and really active, more energetic than many people much younger to her in years. But Jeanie had had a tough life. She had a lot of baggage from her early years. A sister who always picked on her and told her that she was ugly, the fact that she was widowed at a relatively young age, and a tight money situation that was created following the transition of her spouse. The problem was that Jeanie spoke of her past often. Everyone who knows her, knows her story. What do you think that did for her? Yes, it kept the negativity of all those past experiences alive and active inside her – accumulating resistance. After her 70th birthday, which was a big celebration, Jeanie started "realizing" or "feeling" the fact that she was getting on in years. She also started noticing much more than she had done before that many people her age did not have good health. She heard of friends who had had difficult health situations to deal with, and more now than ever, she worried about maintaining good health. All it took was for her to hear of someone who had a stroke or cancer and say to herself "I don't want that" or "I hope I never get that", to accumulate resistance on the subject of health. These seem like the normal thing one would say. And even though the objective is to want a positive outcome, the thought is not a positive thought. In fact, it is a negative thought, because "I hope I never get that" is another way of saying "I am afraid of that". And fear is a negative emotion. Any thought that is connected to a negative emotion is not a positive thought. And so, unknowingly, or in her obliviousness of how the universe works, my friend Jeanie created a stroke.

These thoughts created the weak spot, and all the resistance that was accumulated in the past, used that outlet to release the pressure that had accumulated over the years.

The same question my young friend asked me yesterday "how do people attract negative events they have never thought about?"

We took the example of someone we both knew (I will call him Frank) who had broken his back during a holiday in Mexico, at the age of 35 or there abouts. He was perfectly healthy, and seemingly happy prior to this event – so why did it happen?

Frank had told me himself that he always felt dominated by his father, and that he had low self-confidence. I also know that he was working very long hours in his business – a business that needed timely execution of orders received from clients – a business that operated on precision, where an ill executed order could potentially result in large losses. Frank continuously operated under the pressure of deadlines, and precision. Every order added to the accumulated pressure.

He told me once that it would take him a good couple of days just to shake off the tension and start enjoying his holiday, and then it would be time to go home. Just before he goes on this particular holiday, he puts into place a group health insurance plan for his employees. He doesn't want to be included in the plan, because he never gets sick.

You think he spent some time thinking about and focusing on illness and what happens as a result of it as his insurance rep took him through the process of putting the insurance plan in place? With this back drop, on day two of his holiday, he decides to go surfing. He loves the water, and he is a strong swimmer. But the waves were really high that day, and the one he picked whipped him around and pinned him down – he broke his back. He does not understand why this happened – how did he create this?

First, I think that he already had some resistance accumulated from his childhood, but mostly I think that the tension from his business was still active in his mind – maybe there were orders from clients or other aspects of his business that he was still thinking about having left undone? 30 years later, he doesn't remember very clearly the specifics of the preceding events – what he does remember with extreme clarity is his journey through rehab and back to walking from a complete paralysis waist down. Given the fact that he himself stated that it took him several days to unwind – I'm going to say that the tension of the business was active on holiday day two. There had been some attention given to illness due to the process of putting the insurance into place, creating the weak spot. So the resistance found a crack... It really is that simple.

When something huge like that happen, the tendency is for us to find a reason that is as big – but often times, it is the slow accumulation of tension, and worry on a daily basis, that is unresolved and unreleased that gushes out in the form of a large event.

My friend thought that breaking his back should have been the result of a huge worry, or some other severe mental tension – what he did not realize is that it was the accumulation of a lot of little things, but things/thoughts that occupied the major portion of his daily thoughts – his habit of thought was mostly of worry. He expected more things to go wrong than right, he expected more things to be hard than easy. He expected more people to be careless than careful. The balance of his habit of thought was on the negative side of the equation. My friend Jeanie, thought that she was doing everything to stay in good health and didn't seem to have any major worry in her life at this stage. It wasn't a major worry that caused her stroke. It was the habit of thought of not wanting to be sick. You see, every time you think about not wanting to be sick you are activating the thought of sickness in your mind without realizing it. So in Jeanie's case she was activating a negative thought while wanting a positive result. A habit of thinking that is most destructive. And also one that is most common. If she would instead have just asked for good health and left it at that, she would not have created the stroke.

You see it's the amount of time you spend thinking negative thoughts and not the enormity of the issue you focus on that determines the momentum with which you are propelled towards the negative or the size and magnitude of the negativity that unfolds in your life.

Take my father. He had a massive heart attack in 1985 – he was just 53. He had always been extremely healthy. But there was a history of diabetes in his family, and at the time he was just a little bit over weight. My mother pointed these "facts" out to him as she tried to stir him towards what she considered healthy food choices. Those were the good old days when the media was full of the co-relation between body weight and heart disease. Did a heart attack need to happen? Probably not. I contend that there were many people with a history of diabetes in their family and a bigger weight problem compared to my father who never suffered from a heart attack.

Two things happened in my father's case. First, he had a weak spot, created by the belief that diabetes in the family made him vulnerable to heart disease and that being overweight did the same. Second, he had a spouse who was a worrier and insisted in keeping active in both their vibrations all the tension and worry of events and people under the category of "organizational politics". Was he thinking specifically about getting a heart attack? I don't think so – but the weak spot was there and the tension was there... and the rest as they say is history.

Things you don't want don't have to happen – there don't have to be any surprises in your life – if you stay in touch with your emotional guidance.

When we think a thought that is not in our best interest, for a split second we feel the tinge of emotion that lets us know that that thought carried resistance. Most people are so used to brushing away this vital information and moving on with other thoughts that they don't take notice. Over a period of time, we get so used to feeling negative emotion and brushing it away that it becomes habit to suppress negative emotion – creating a disconnect with our natural guidance system. It's never too late to mending the disconnect. Soon as you make the decision that you want to start paying attention to your emotional guidance – you will. If you continue to put forth your intention to listen to your emotional guidance over a period of time you will not only mend the disconnect, you will in fact make your ability to interpret that inner guidance much stronger.

My advice to all: clean up your vibration, and select your words and your thoughts carefully. **You are the one who picks the thoughts that you think – so do yourself a favor – think thoughts that will serve you well.**

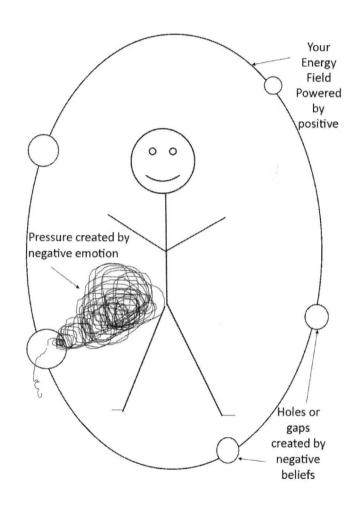

Your Energy Field Powered by positive

Pressure created by negative emotion

Holes or gaps created by negative beliefs

If you don't mind my drawing, the diagram above illustrates what I want to share.

Our positive beliefs create a sort of force field around us that doesn't let bad stuff get into our personal vibrational space, or realm. When we hear someone say something that is less than empowering, such as, "research shows that the likelihood of getting allergies in the spring is higher because of pollen in the air", and we say "really? If research has proven it – it must be true". Now, we have accepted this as true and therefore it creates a crack (of least resistance), or hole in our force field.

Now let's say you go to a party and meet someone who says, "I have terrible allergies just now – it's all that pollen in the air". "Ah!" you say "that research must be right". Now you have made that crack in your force field a little bigger.

Every time you come across evidence that upholds the belief about pollen allergies (which of course you will, because the law of attraction will bring you more things that match up with what you believe), that little hole will keep getting bigger and bigger and bigger.

All the resistance that you have been accumulating, not just on one subject but a whole medley of things that have been minor every day irritancies for you, will find release through the biggest hole in your force field. Make sense?

It is at this stage that my friends get confused. The confusion arises from the fact that they had never thought of themselves as negative thinkers. They have no idea how to start identifying which thoughts are negative and how to rephrase them. How to start using language that is empowering and positive. How to consciously give up beliefs that are negative.

Here is one way to identify your habit of thought.

When you think of something that you want or some event that you want to have happen, do you ask yourself: how is it going to ...? when is it going to...? who is going to...? where is it going to...? Do you use these questions as conversation starters with yourself and then paint endless scenarios in your mind about how things can work out? Do you ask the questions how? When? Who? Where? Repeatedly. If you answered "yes" then my dear friend, you have work to do, because this sort of thinking pattern is indicative of a self-sabotaging habit of thought.

Tension, worry, anxiety, fear are all negative emotions – don't brush them under the carpet. Acknowledge them. Acknowledge the guidance that is telling you that you have taken the wrong fork in the road, in terms of thinking and perhaps even in terms of doing.

When you catch yourself thinking this way – stop. Acknowledge that you do not have to think these thoughts right now, this red hot minute. In this minute "All is well". Trust that there are endless possibilities and many that you could not possibly be aware of. Admit that you do not have control over all the variables involved in things working out your way – but the one thing you do control is how you think your thoughts. Say to yourself, that you want to choose positive thoughts and develop an empowering habit of thought – and you will.

One of the things I like to do is to ask the question "Why?" Why do I want this thing that I want? Why do I want things to happen in a certain way. The answer to the question Why? always takes you to the positive side of the thinking equation.

The thinking equation:

Positive	Negative
Why do I want this?	How? When? Who? Where?

Sometimes people want to change their habit of thought but they find that they can't control their way of thinking. This is simply because thoughts have momentum. **Once you get a sort of thinking habit going it gathers speed, and this makes it difficult to stop.**

It's Ok to keep working on it slowly, whenever you can, and you will notice that as you make the conscious effort to change, that change will come. It's like trying to turn an ocean liner around to make it go in another direction. First you have to bring it to a stop – slowly –then turn it around, and keep going until it starts gathering speed in the new direction. So be easy on yourself. If you want it – it will come.

Thought always comes before action. So there is no need to act, unless the action will bring you respite, and make you feel better.

When people start this work with me, often times they expect that they should go from a zero on the Happy Scale to a ten (ten being best), and then stay there. When that doesn't happen, they discard the law of attraction and the science of deliberate creation – because they don't see the evidence of it working.

What they do not know is that, feeling respite, feeling just a little bit better than before is in fact evidence that more good stuff is on it's way. What they do not know is that hardly anyone can maintain a consistent 10 on the Happy Scale, every minute of the day, day in, day out. We all experience various levels on the Happy Scale during a day – success is in acknowledging when you are below 10 and then doing the work that makes you feel just a little bit better so that the direction in which you are travelling is upwards, towards joy.

In my book The Prosperity Puzzle, I teach a technique that helps to accelerate the process of bringing your habit of thought towards the positive side. In summary, this technique involves three steps:

First, state it the way it is. Second, find something about the way things are that is positive and absolutely true. Third, make a clear statement of improvement, not a drastic improvement, just a step or two towards getting to where you want to go. You can repeat this three step process as many times as you like. All we want to accomplish with this technique is to feel incrementally better. No need to look for physical evidence of improvement – just trust that if you are doing the work then the evidence will come. Make sense?

Everything that we want in life is because by the having of it we want to feel good.

Even when you want to help someone, you want it because through it you will feel good. When you make what you call a sacrifice, by giving up something that you have in order to help someone else, you do so because in the doing of it you will feel better than in the holding back of it. And it is so with everything in life.

Therefore, the purpose of life is Joy, experiencing happiness.

Here is a little diagram to help illustrate how the science of deliberate creation works.

We experience the world and identify what we want. When we identify what we do not want – the flip side of it is always what we do want.

Not getting the object of our desire makes us feel the contrast of not having it more strongly and so another desire is born. In order for the desire to be fulfilled we must have an attitude of ease about it. An attitude of ease means that we are not thinking thoughts that put us on the negative side of the thinking equation. Being on the negative side of the equation leads to another unfulfilled desire, and so on. When this happens we get the feeling of being "stuck".

Have you ever noticed how some couples try really hard to have a baby for many years. Then they "give-up" or they adopt – next thing you know they have a baby of their own on the way. A very dear colleague of mine and his wife were a prime example, and over the years I have heard of so many similar stories – I am sure you have too.

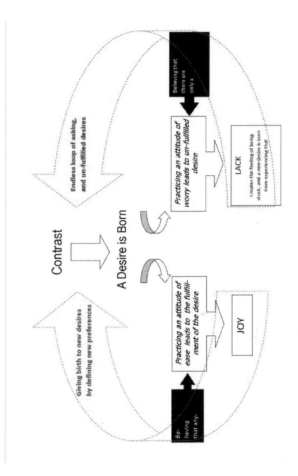

Contrast

A Desire is Born

Endless loop of asking, and un-fulfilled desires

Giving birth to new desires by defining new preferences

Believing that there are only a

Practicing an attitude of worry leads to un-fulfilled desire

LACK
Creates the feeling of being stuck, and a new desire is born from experiencing that

Practicing an attitude of ease leads to the fulfil-ment of the desire

JOY

Be-lieving that any-

23

What is at work there? There is a desire for a child. The desire is not fulfilled. Every time the couple tries for a baby and is unsuccessful they give birth to a new desire. Then they give-up, which creates an attitude of ease and the desire is fulfilled.

But wait, the unanswered question here is what got in the way of allowing it the first time around? Some people might have thought that conceiving a baby was not the easiest of things to do. But what if there was no such thought in the minds of Ray and Sue? If they had never had a negative thought about the subject – then what happened? As in the case of my friend Jeanie, my Father and my friend Frank, it wasn't a negative thought about the subject of having a baby itself, but negativity on other subjects that could have accumulated and found a weak spot in the emotional make-up of either one or both Ray and Sue.

Our discussion can evolve from here and go in so many other directions. But I think this is a good place to stop. I would like to encourage everyone reading this book to take a quick inventory of things you want that have been stuck and not happening for a while and decide to do one of two things about them. Either move on, give-up, make peace or work on creating ease and flow in your life with respect to them. When you achieve a habit of thought that comes from a place of ease and flow your life becomes magical, and there is never any need to worry about anything ever again – and that is a very good place to be!

Blessings.

Zehra

About the author

Zehra Mahoon lives in Ontario, Canada with her two beautiful children, Kinza and Faris, a hyper cat called Izzy, a lazy cat called Sitka and Stella the forever puppy.

Zehra loves her small town Oshawa and over the past fourteen years she has finally adjusted to the snow and cold weather in Ontario, but always welcomes a timely opportunity to get away to warmer places preferably with lots of old trees, rocks and water, good food and vibrant colours.

Zehra teaches weekly meditation classes at the local library and offers an open discussion session. She loves to teach, coach and write for her blog, as well as other journals and magazines. Zehra is an accomplished speaker and often makes television appearances. Aside from teaching the law of attraction, and offering financial advice , Zehra loves to cook and entertain and have fun with each new day of her life. To find out more about Zehra and her work please visit her website at zmahoon.com.

Zehra's other books include:

Thrive – Free yourself from Worry, Anger and other negative emotions

Thrive!

Free Yourself from Worry, Anger
and Other Negative Emotions

By Zehra Mahoon

Many books have been written about anger management and over coming worry and anxiety and about what to think and believe and how to act, but three things set this book apart from the rest:

1. The depiction of the thinking process in the form of illustrations that make it easy to understand how our thoughts impact our results;

2. A method that helps us to identify the beliefs that operate under the surface and control our lives without our knowing it; and

3. A simple four step process that helps to deactivate negative beliefs permanently so that we can thrive.

The end result: freedom from worry, anxiety, and anger and a set of thinking exercises that can be used in every situation you would ever encounter in life.

How to pray so that God listens – 100
prayers for ultimate joy & success in life

HOW TO PRAY SO
THAT GOD LISTENS

100 PRAYERS FOR ULTIMATE
JOY & SUCCESS IN LIFE

ZEHRA MAHOON

- What is a prayer?
- Is prayer a useless ritual?
- Why should I pray?
- Will I get all the things I want if I pray?
- Is there a right and wrong way to pray?
- Does God answer all prayers?
- Why do people who never pray get what they want, and those who pray don't?
- What does Ask and it is Given really mean?
- What should a prayer include?
- Is there a good or bad time to pray?
- Why are some prayers answered quickly and others take a long time?
- Why do some people get everything they want and others don't?
- Does religion make a difference to the effectiveness of prayer?
- Is God really fair?
- Does God really love me?
- Why do bad things happen to good people?
- Can I really put my trust in God?
- Can I control the outcomes in my life?
- Can I improve my life and be truly happy?
- Can I truly have, be and do anything I want?

These and many other questions are answered in these pages.

Is this Apple from my Tree? is a book about parenting.

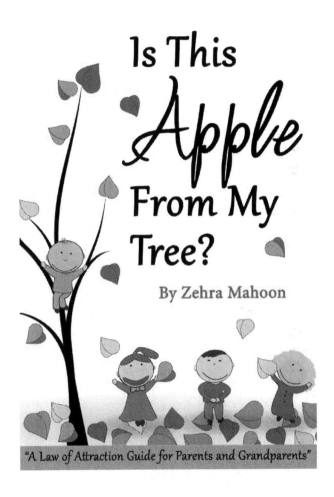

Is This *Apple* From My Tree?

By Zehra Mahoon

"A Law of Attraction Guide for Parents and Grandparents"

Being a good parent is as much about looking after yourself as it is about looking after your child.

This book will help you to:

1. Become a confident, relaxed and happy parent who enjoys every moment of having children.

2. Raise children with positive belief systems that enable them to be confident, happy, healthy, creative, and successful.

Zehra shares many practical examples of situation that she encountered with her own children how she dealt with them successfully to help you understand how your power of positive thinking impacts your children without ever having to tell them to change or do anything differently.

Peace Within is a book about meditation

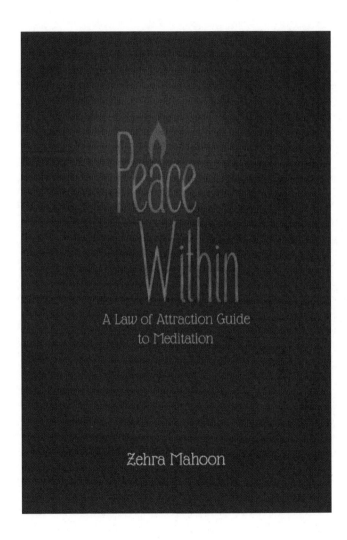

Meditation is made out to be way more difficult than it truly is. One of the reasons for this is that there are so many different ways being taught. The purpose of this little book is to dig down to the foundation of the process of meditation and talk about why things are done in various different ways. The fewer the rules and rituals the easier it is.

This book makes meditation easy.

If you have wanted to learn meditation and felt that you could not turn off your thoughts then this book is meant for you for you are about to learn that there is really no need for you to ever turn your thoughts off – in fact you can't – that's the equivalent of telling your heart to stop pumping blood!

The Prosperity Puzzle: Your relationship with money and how to improve it

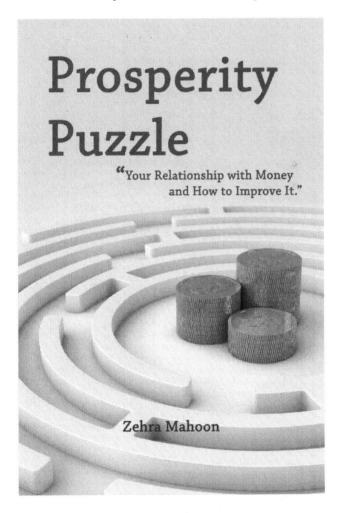

Have you ever wondered why some people who have the skills and the education and everything else they need to be successful aren't and others who have far less qualifications are?

Have you ever wondered why one business in the same industry with the same product succeeds and another doesn't?

That's what this book is all about – it explains how the way we think about money has an impact upon how much money flows into our lives.

It explains how to work on and remove the negative beliefs that are standing between you and prosperity. You deserve to be rich, and anything that you want is possible.

Win: a law of attraction guide to winning

A LAW OF ATTRACTION
GUIDE TO WINNING
THE LOTTERY

ZEHRA
MAHOON

The Law of Attraction is always working, whether you use it consciously or not.

This powerful law is at the base of why things out the way they do.

This book will help you to improve your understanding of the nine important elements that contribute towards winning anything – especially the lottery, accompanied with step wise guide to making them work for you.

This book will give you an understanding of what you need to stop doing in order to start winning the lottery and so much more.

Zehra's books are available in digital and print formats through <u>Amazon.com</u>

One Last Thing...

If you enjoyed this book or found it useful I would truly appreciate it if you would post a short review on Amazon. Your support really does make a difference and I read all the reviews personally so I can get your feedback and make this book even better.

Much love and appreciation,

Zehra

Made in the USA
Las Vegas, NV
15 April 2022

47508291R00026